DIVO
FOR BEG

DIVORCE
FOR BEGINNERS
How to Get Unhitched Without the Hitches

CATHY HOPKINS
CARTOONS BY GRAY JOLLIFFE

HarperCollins*Publishers*

HarperCollins*Publishers*,
77–85 Fulham Palace Road,
Hammersmith, London W6 8JB

Published by HarperCollins*Publishers* 1995
1 3 5 7 9 8 6 4 2

A catalogue record for this book is
available from the British Library

ISBN 0 00 638443 9

Set in Linotron ITC Garamond and Futura by
Rowland Phototypesetting Limited,
Bury St Edmunds, Suffolk

Printed in Great Britain by
HarperCollinsManufacturing Glasgow

CONTENTS

PART THREE

HAPPY ENDINGS

INTRODUCTION

Why is this divorce survival guide for beginners? Because if you're already divorced, chances are you won't have the money to buy this book.

But divorce doesn't have to ruin you. You don't have to end up bitter enemies.

It can be a happy occasion, an event you can cherish for the rest of your lives.

Alimony doesn't always mean acrimony and there's no law that says you can't remain friends. Divorce can be as painless or as painful as you want to make it. It's just a matter of going about it in the right frame of mind and remembering that where there's give and take, it's usually the lawyers who do the taking.

Read this book and do it the easy way – it'll be OK in the end, even if you are the one that gets stuck with the kids.

PART 1

I DO . . . NOT

1

IS IT REALLY OVER?

> *There is one thing I would break up over and that's if she caught me with another woman. I won't stand for that*
>
> *Steve Martin*

Before starting divorce proceedings, are you sure it's really over? Might the trouble blow over, be a misunderstanding that'll pass, bringing you together again, closer than ever? So you found her in bed with your father? Every relationship has its ups and downs.

Before reading on, try this simple questionnaire to determine how you really feel.

1) After the last time you made love, your partner:
a) cuddled you and chatted for a while
b) went straight to sleep
c) came home early and nearly caught you
d) drew around the outline of your body with chalk, then called the mortuary

2) You find your partner in bed with your best friend:
a) Just thinking of it makes you so jealous, you

    realize you still have strong feelings for them

b) It makes you realize you're partly to blame and should have made more effort to keep your love life alive

c) You're concerned for your friend

3) Your partner isn't home by three a.m., you:
a) Start phoning the hospitals and police
b) Can't sleep listening for their car or footsteps
c) Wouldn't notice as it's their turn to baby-sit the following night

4) If you imagine your partner dead in a car accident:
a) It makes you realize how much you love him
b) It makes you wish you hadn't argued the last time you saw her
c) It makes you wish you'd thought of it sooner

If you answered a or b to any of these, it is clear that there is still a chance you'll pull through. Where there's an ember, there can still be a fire. Go back to book four, *Keeping It Up – How to Make Your Love Affair Last Forever*.

    If you answered c to all the questions, *Divorce for Beginners* is the book for you, so read on before you do serious damage or get arrested.

    And forget about embers and fire, you shouldn't be allowed near matches for a while.

So just what are the signs that a marriage is really over?

    Q: How can you tell when your wife's dead?
    A: The sex is the same but the dishes pile up.

YOU KNOW IT'S OVER WHEN

- The only thing you have in common is that you were both married on the same day
- He calls out yet another name when you're making love
- You call his office, his secretary says he's out at lunch . . . with his wife
- You don't have arguments because that would mean speaking to each other
- You call her office, her secretary says she's out celebrating her pregnancy. You had the snip three years ago

THE TELL-TALE SIGNS THAT SAY ITS ALL OVER :

1) Your wife is living in Tasmania with someone else.

2) She spelt your name wrong.

- You confide in your nanny that you suspect that your husband is having an affair, she goes bright red and says she doesn't believe you
- He phones to say he'll be late for supper, you've already left a note saying dinner's in the dog
- Every time you sit on his knee for a cuddle, he starts dictating
- He says he spent the night with his brother, you know he's lying because you did
- You boast to the au pair that your husband dresses well, she replies, 'yes and so quickly'
- Something's missing in your life. Then you find out your wife moved to Milwaukee six months ago
- When you told her there was someone else, she was genuinely pleased for you

- You can tell exactly when he's lying. His lips move
- Multiple orgasm becomes multiple sarcasm

> The romance is dead if he drinks champagne from your slipper and chokes on a Dr Scholl's foot pad
>
> *Phyllis Diller*

> Basically my wife was immature. I'd be at home in the bath and she'd come in and sink my boats
>
> *Woody Allen*

FALSE SIGNS

If it's only occasionally that your partner drives you to distraction, only sometimes they annoy you like mad with those irritating little habits that you can't stand, like the way she picks at her nails or the way he eats, hey, that's just living in close proximity. Buy some earplugs and turn the other way.

Everyone has periods where they don't love or even like their partner, sometimes it can last for ages but often it's a time when they don't like much else either and the boss is giving them a hard time at work.

Spend a weekend with a close friend for a change and see if absence makes the heart grow fonder.

Temporary strains that may feel like the last straw –

redundancy, illness, worry, pressure at work, a new baby who cries a lot, or a one-night stand – can be outlived. In time, things will feel good again.

Do what you can to improve the external situation and give yourself some time, then see if your relationship improves.

And remember, if you're unhappy, let your partner know so that at least they have the chance to DO something to make it better.

If you know something's got to give, got to change, then before you charge into divorce proceedings it may be worth looking into what other alternatives there are first. Murder or suicide are a little drastic but it may well be that all you need is a break, to relearn how to communicate, to re-evaluate your relationship.

> *SHE: We have to re-evaluate our relationship*
> *HE: I already did, I get a ten, you get a six*
>   *Woody Allen*

ALTERNATIVE SOLUTIONS BEFORE YOU MAKE THE BREAK

Right	*Wrong*
Professional help	The Lorena Bobbitt method
Couple counselling	Hitting the bottle
Time apart	Years apart
A new interest	A new lover

> *I knew a guy, he had heart attacks so he*
> *got a pacemaker. His wife divorced him*
> *because she said it interefered with the TV*
> *Walther Matthau to Jack Lemmon in*
>   *Buddy, Buddy*

Divorce is a big step to take. Have you thought:

- Divorce is expensive. It costs a lot to be free
- Divorce doesn't guarantee happiness
- Kids want you both there, even if you argue
- You won't be able to see the kids as much
- Maybe a stranger will bring up your children (but maybe you feel no one could be stranger than your ex)
- Someone else will be with your spouse
- You may lose the lifestyle you're used to

- You will still argue about money and kids
- You may feel lonely

DON'T do it if it's a case of:

- I don't like myself at the moment. So I'm going to divorce you
- I'm bored. So I'm going to divorce you
- I want a reaction from you. So I'm going to start divorce proceedings

Here's a few of the reasons some of the divorcees I talked to gave as the last straws for them.

HOW DID YOU KNOW IT WAS OVER?

He said

There was this other bloke in our bed

She opened a separate bank account with all my money

She thought our lodger was the coming Messiah

Different bedrooms after rows/Different bedrooms before a row/Different bedrooms, different postal codes

She put a knife through my flying jacket. Luckily I wasn't in it at the time

She stacked my records on the radiator

When I woke up *every* morning wishing I was somewhere else

At our wedding, when it was time to throw the bouquet, she threw it in the bin instead of at the bridesmaids

I knew it was over when I saw her chewing gum and smoking on our first date but I married her and lived with her for years anyway

By the look on her face when I told her of my hundredth extra-marital liaison

A candlewick dressing gown and a badly executed perm

I met a 44 DD blonde with an attitude that was the total opposite of my wife's

When we started telling each other the whole truth. Never a good idea

I came home, everything had gone

She said

It was doomed from the beginning but I chose to ignore the signs

Couldn't stand his smell, the way he ate, the way he walked, what he said

When he broke my nose

Couldn't bear him to touch me

I discovered he was taking drugs with a quarter of the city, sleeping with half of the city and lying to all of it

He preferred to make love to himself than to me

2

BREAKING THE NEWS

> *My husband wanted a room of his own.*
> *He wanted it in Pittsburgh*
>
> *Phyllis Diller*

If you've decided to go ahead with it, next you have to tell your partner.

HOW TO BREAK THE NEWS

One woman, when asked to bring something she didn't want to the Ladies' Guild White Elephant Stall, brought her husband. Not the most subtle of techniques but it made the point. Everybody knows how you ought to do it – sit your partner down and just come out with it. Be honest. Be cruel to be kind. Don't draw it out or give false hope. She asks what you want for your birthday – you reply 'a divorce'. Clean, simple and well, she did ask.

And pigs may fly if I ever meet anyone who's actually done it that way. Most of us, being emotional cowards at heart, don't like to hurt or be hurt and so go for major avoidance tactics for as long as possible, until the situation becomes unbearable. Then it's time for one of the following:

TEN POSSIBLE WAYS TO SAY GOODBYE

1) The slow and tortuous

'I DO still love you, only . . . , but . . . , and . . . , also . . . , I know, I know . . . . , so many memories, so much shared, good times, bad times, we rode them all, Christmases, birthdays, holidays, the children . . . By the way, this is Olga'

2) Avoidance and redirected blame

'It wasn't you, it was me'

'I couldn't stand your mother'

'I couldn't live with your nagging/scratching/snoring'

'It was the cats. I know there's nothing wrong with cats but all over the bed?'

3) The Lord Lucan

Kill the nanny and just disappear. A bit drastic, but effective.

4) The Insensitive

'I'm off. And you're not coming'

5) The Cruel

'I'm off, you're not coming. And I always faked my erections/ orgasms'

6) The Greta Garbo

– I wanna be alone

'Yeah, OK not exactly alone. Yeah. Monique will be with me. What I mean by alone is the not-with-you type of alone'

7) You're the Last One to Know

Her mother phones and says 'Oh you're still there?!'

8) Hedging your Bets

(Not burning your bridges in case the next one doesn't work out.)

'We can still be friends. You'll always be very special to me . . . but not that special at the moment . . . but you might be

again. Don't forget me. Let's have a coffee and stay in touch (in case Gianni finds a younger version and deserts me in a few years' time)'

9) The Sarcastic

Your wife tells you that she's going to pose for a picture of Eve and the snake and you ask who's going to be Eve.

10) The Cowardly

a) Leaving clues: you're too chicken to end it, but you've been having an affair for years and secretly want to get found out so you get careless about covering your tracks. Hopefully your partner'll spot the clues and do the dumping for you.

b) by letter, or better still by fax.

Dear Martha, I have run off with the barmaid from The Bag and Badger. Love Eric

And if you don't know what to write, you haven't got the words, send a goodbye card. Here are some suggestions that should convey the message and are my version of the schmaltzy divorce cards that are now for sale in the States and are coming here soon.

Loving you was
- like Christmas telly – boring and repetitive
- leaving me speechless – it wasn't worth talking about
- like thunder – a quick bang and it was over
- like driving a Rolls-Royce – flat out all I could hear was the clock ticking
- like a case of champagne – a real headache
- making me feel like a million dollars – have your chequebook handy
- like nothing I've experienced before – exceptionally dull
- a spiritual experience – it took nine vodkas to face you

> *Anne Boleyn: Not tonight I've got a headache*
> *Henry VIII: We'll soon fix that*
>
> *Mike Harding*

Those fateful lines that said 'Love is over'

- Get 'im Rover
- I'm having a baby. No, not *your* baby
- What's your name again?
- Yeah well fuck you too
- Grow up!
- Give me my credit cards back
- I would like us to stay friends
- I thought it was forever, and that's what it seemed like

This is how some of the divorcees I spoke to broke the good news.

HOW DID YOU LET YOUR PARTNER KNOW OR VICE VERSA?

He said

By post from another country

The coward's way out. I told my partner I needed to be by myself a while to sort myself out – nothing to do with her, blah, blah, it was my problem.

'Why don't you fuck right off?'

By not coming home . . . for a few years

She took our bed to the flat she now shares with her new lover

Working late and coming home smelling of perfume with my back covered in scratches

She said

He was issued with a High Court Ouster order. Seemed a pretty effective way

Starting looking for another flat

WHAT WOULD BE AN IDEAL WAY?

He said

Her and her mother killed in plane crash leaving me a fortune

Ask them what they want out of the relationship, tell them what you want. If the answers don't add up, *arrivederci*.

Getting caught in a frenzied orgy with six page three girls

From the bottom of the garden then run like billy-ho

Letting her go over Bristol Suspension Bridge

Messages on a banner across the M25 at every junction, dear . . . my lawyer's number is . . .

She said

Get divorced immediately while they're still guilty

There's no ideal way

Have him killed

He sits down and says sorry it's over but here's two million and a holiday in the Caribbean as compensation

And when that's over, there's still friends and family to tell.

> *When a couple decide to divorce, they should inform both sets of parents before having a party and telling all their friends. This is not only courteous but practical. Parents may be very willing to pitch in with comments, criticism and malicious gossip of their own to help the divorce along*
>
> P.J. O'Rourke, Modern Manners

FRIENDS

Friends are easier to tell than family and will usually take sides immediately and slag off the partner you thought they liked with amazing enthusiasm.

Her way of telling friends

FEMALE DIVORCEE: I'm getting divorced. It's over between me and Tim.

FRIEND: Gosh, you must be feeling devastated. Let me have his phone number.

His way of telling friends

MALE DIVORCEE: See Arsenal lost on Saturday
and I dumped Annie.
FRIEND: Yeah. Wanna beer?

PARENTS

Most people dread going to their parents with the news. Immediately you're ten years old again and taking home a lousy school report with all D-s on it.

'Mary could do better if she put her mind to it.'
'James hasn't really tried.'

But it may not be as bad as you think. For years, your parents have probably not been needed. You're grown up now, adult and can manage on your own. But now you need them and they may just welcome the chance to be useful again.

Many divorcees are pleasantly surprised at the support and understanding they get from their old-fashioned mas and pas.

But then again, they may cut you out of their will and side with your ex.

What can be confusing is once the tears have been dried, the cups of tea made and drunk, friends and family just *have* to chip in with a bit of advice. And none of it the same.

MUM: Stay friends
FRIEND: Bin the bastard

DAD: Come to a fair settlement
FRIEND: Screw 'im for all he's got

FRIEND: You deserve better
MUM: You should have tried harder. It takes two

FRIEND: You could still find a partner. You still look good
MUM: You let yourself go, no wonder she left

MUM: I never liked her
DAD: You'll be hard pushed to find another like her, try and work things out between you

DAD: You were too good for him
FRIEND: He thought he was too good for you

MUM: Find another committed relationship and
settle down again
FRIEND: Screw around for a bit, have a bit of fun

FRIEND: You need quiet time to heal
MOTHER: Keep busy

Aaaaghhhhhhhhhhhh. It can go on and on but they mean
well. The best thing in the early stages is to take it day by day.
Your feelings are going to fluctuate, and how!

I blame myself for the tragic death of my husband.
Oh, why's that?
I shot him.

And if *you* are a friend or relation of someone splitting up with the partner, DON'T:

Arrange a blind date with Ned from the office who has never had a girlfriend but has a kind heart

Try to arrange a reconciliation on *Surprise, Surprise*

3

ALONE AGAIN

> *I feel so miserable without you, it's almost*
> *like having you here*
> *Stephen Bishop, song title*

Finding yourself on your own again after having been in a partnership will obviously take some adjusting to. Whether dumper or dumpee, it's still a loss for both concerned.

It's rare that both parties agree at the same time and are happy about the split. More often there's one who initiates the break-up and one who would have gone on and tried to weather the storm. So there's the dumper and the dumpee, the guilty and the rejected.

Sometimes dumpers don't express what they're feeling because of guilt and dumpees don't express what they're feeling for fear of ruining any chance of reconciliation. So both are very nice and very depressed.

Whichever you are, don't expect just to sail through it as if you'll be the one who is unaffected, won't be touched. You may even miss your partner even though you could no longer stand them.

> *I'm still missing my husband.*
> *But my aim is getting better*

According to the many therapists who work with divorcees, everyone is affected to greater or lesser degrees and apparently the stages of grief after a break-up are pretty standard. My divorcee friend Gill thinks they can be summed up in four words – madness, moaning, moping and mending. But for argument's sake, let's take a look at what the experts say.

STAGES OF GRIEF

Denial

Not believing it's over. The refusal to face up to the fact that the relationship is finished and it hurts like hell.

Anger

This happens when you can't work the denial bit anymore.

Revenge

This can give you your first opportunity since adolescence to act irresponsibly and possibly get away with it. Go for it. It's part of the healing process. Send the love letters that your ex wrote you to your new rival or take a tip from something I saw in a soap opera – keep sending your ex taxis, pizzas and Indian takeaways that they never ordered.

Blame

Basically it goes like this: 'I'm bloody perfect and loveable. The break down of the relationship is your fault. Everything is your fault. Even World War Two.'

Apparently this shows immaturity and an unwillingness to be adult and take responsibility for contributing to the break-up. But I'm sure if you go deep enough and do a bit of soul-searching, you'll soon find someone else to blame for giving you that kind of attitude in the first place, like your parents or your teacher.

This stage may also involve phone calls to friends and family to 'get them on your side'. 'I behaved perfectly, it all went wrong because of my ex. Are you with me or shall I take your name off my Christmas card list now?'

Incessant talk about ex

Though boring for your friends, it shows the need to let what's happening sink in and become a reality. Only then can you deal with it properly.

Be prepared for outrageous phone bills.

Fear

> *I have a new philosophy. I'm only going to dread one day at a time*
> *Charles Schulz,* Peanuts *cartoon*

Once it has sunk in, panic may result. A whole host of bogeymen will appear in the back of your head, each with his own version on 'How will you cope?'

'You're going to die alone'

'You'll never get laid again'

'You're too old'

'You're losing your mind'

'You keep reading things twice, a sure sign you're losing your mind'

'You keep reading things twice, a sure sign you're losing your mind'

The bogeys say mad things, they say scarey things. Tell them all to go to hell. They're not real, they're only bogeymen for grown-ups and NOT to be taken at all seriously.

Shock

People in shock sometimes do really daft things. Another good excuse to behave badly and get away with it.

Confusion

You've lost a partner, companion, role, lifestyle, security and even though you were miserable with them, it can take courage to make that first step towards a new life. Like the bird that is freed but hesitates before it flies because its prison had become familiar.

In a marriage, it's so easy to hand over so much of one's identity, stop going out, lose touch with friends.

How many times do we hear couples describing their partner as their other half or better half, like they're incomplete without them. Like they've become some alien two headed being. No wonder it's confusing when you find yourself alone again. Suddenly you have to find your lost half. It's like separating Siamese twins. You don't know who you are anymore. You're not so-and-so's wife or husband anymore. You're just plain ole whatsit again. ANOTHER good excuse for bad behaviour.

Distorted memories –
only remembering the good times

Even though you couldn't be alone in the same room as your ex for years, suddenly it's the middle of the night, you're feeling blue and your song comes on the radio. You remember the way he used to make you laugh with his version of a Hawaiian doing the hoola hoola dance and the next thing you know, you're wishing he was back.

The only way to get through these times of nostalgia and sentimentality is to change the radio station and get out your 'what I hated about my ex' list.

Some helpful reminders to see you through the early days:

The main areas to focus on are:

- Disgusting personal habits: fingers in orifices where they don't belong sort of habits, eg: picking out navel debris during *Cheers* and examining it absentmindedly
- Eating habits: eating with the mouth open and trying to talk at the same time, slurpy, chompy, wet, chewy noises with dribbling, missing the mouth and getting food on the chin
- Unattractive physical trait, easy for women:

Even if he was the handsomest chap in the world, think scrotum. Think of him bending over, away from you, that astonishing sight of dingley dangley testicles. As Billy Connolly said, on the heavenly conveyor belt where the angels were making humans, they'd been working on the elbows and had bits of skin left over. God told them to put the 'bits' out of the way, in a corner where they wouldn't be seen and bingo, testicles. From the right angle they look like something nasty that has crawled out of a chap's bum. Oh yes, those turkey giblet bits'll put you off any sentimental daydreaming.

For him, think stretch marks, think saggy, baggy, crepey bits. Bits that have started the long journey south no matter how much she scrubbed away at herself with her herbal skin toning gloop in the bathroom.

'I'll never forget the smell of your sweat, under your armpits.' Magic moments.

- Bad sex: Remember his seductive foreplay and the way he used to whisper 'brace yourself'. His idea of romance was to open his beer can away from your face.

  Remember the time she said 'let me know when you've finished, the movie's on in a minute.'

- Money: His tightness. The way he'd buy cheap wine and stick on an expensive label thinking you didn't know.

  Her extravagance: the way she'd buy expensive wine and stick on a cheap label thinking you'd never know.

- Disgusting infections your ex couldn't get rid of: a rash of his football friends, a dose of her dreadful sisters.

> *The husband was a teetotaller, there was no other woman. The conduct complained of was that he had drifted into the habit of winding up every meal by taking out his false teeth and hurling them at his wife*
> *Arthur Conan Doyle,* A Case of Identity

Bargaining

Be careful if thinking about bargaining. In a weak moment, you may think, 'come back I'll change'. But you probably mean 'come back *you'll* change'. But they don't. And after a few days you suddenly remember what you hated about them in the first place.

Loneliness

Can be the worst feeling of all. Call on friends, invite family to stay, best of all get a pet, a cat or a dog. You'll never have a more faithful friend.

> *I never married because there was no need. I have three pets at home that answer the same purpose as a husband. I have a dog that growls in the morning, a parrot that swears all afternoon and a cat that comes home late at night*
>
> Marie Corelli

Guilt

Complete turn around from the beginning when your ex was to blame for everything. Now you believe it's all *your* fault and *you're* the unloveable one.

A loss of confidence at some stage or other is inevitable. You start to think those things that the ex said in the heat of the moment may be true and in troop another coachload of bogeys. Distant cousins of the 'fear bogeys', this lot come out with their own style of hogwash and most of it starts with 'if only you had . . . '

'If only you'd made more effort . . . '

'If only you'd gone along with him and tried group sex in rubber thongs with the Nesbitt family over the road.'

'If only you'd bought that video *The Lovers' Guide to Sex* instead of *Terminator*'

Don't listen. No one's perfect. We all make mistakes. If suddenly everyone in the world starts to look as though they've got it together and you're the only one who's failed, failed, failed, imagine them on the toilet.

Depression

> *He's turned his life around. He used to be*
> *depressed and miserable. Now he's*
> *miserable and depressed*
>
> *David Frost*

Some days you've just got to give in, go under and be depressed. Many people have many cures and advice to give but why bother? You can try 'em all later when you're feeling better.

Divorce is a shitty business, there's going to be some rocky days. Pull down the blinds, have a good cry, don't speak to anyone for days, drink too much. In fact why not accelerate the process and listen to Leonard Cohen's early records.

It's not easy breaking up. No one will blame you for being low.

Except your ex of course.

Letting go

> *We should forgive our enemies but only*
> *after they've been hanged first*
>
> *Heinrich Heine*

Asking someone to 'let go' too soon in divorce proceedings is like asking someone hanging on with one hand to a thirtieth-floor windowledge to let go.

Don't bother even thinking about it, no matter how often well-intentioned friends say the words.

One morning, you'll wake up and it will just have happened.

The fact that it may well be the same morning that you wake up after your first night of wild abandoned sex with a new lover is purely coincidental.

Transition

The stage you reach when you've stopped blaming your partner and want to understand why the relationship ended so that you don't make the same mistakes again.

It is also the term given to the stage in childbirth when the mother-to-be goes off her head and starts shouting abuse at everyone she sees. Try not to get the two confused because you've had your go at that earlier on in the process and are meant to have moved on by now.

Regaining identity/trust/sexuality

This may also be the same morning after the night of the steamy sex.

Acceptance

You're starting to feel OK and up for strutting about saying things like 'Frankly my dear, I don't give a damn.'

You mean it.

> Have you ever noticed how people whose marriages are breaking up keep redecorating the kitchen?
>
> Matthew Paris

Other symptoms you may encounter along the way are:

Weight loss	Not sleeping
Weight gain	Sleeping too much
Lack of interest in sex	Listlessness
Heightened horniness	Hyperactivity
Rapid mood changes	Suicidal feelings
Consistent low	Tremendous highs

Oh plus various assorted psychosomatic illnesses – headaches, colitis, asthma, ulcers and stress.

It's no wonder confusion is big on the list! But if you can get through all this, the chances are you will be ready to embark on a new relationship and benefit from the understanding you have acquired along the way.

Except that the fact that you are now so wise means that's the last thing you'd dream of doing.

Although the stages of grief are similar, different personalities will deal with the road to recovery in their own ways. There's the drama queen, the recluse, the noble and tragic, the philosophical, the jubilant, the hopeless, the desperate, the bitter, the 'let's be friends' and finally the pro who knows the ropes so well he has a season ticket down at the courts.

Some people say it takes two years to recover from a divorce so give yourself time and be prepared for setbacks, songs, reminders. Find time to cry, let it out. Don't pester your ex for reassurance and certainly don't ever, *ever* sleep with them.

Here's how some of the 'panel' dealt with it.

HOW DID YOU REACT DURING AND AFTER THE BREAK UP?

Drank a lot, smoked a lot, went temporarily mad – others would say no change

With anger, frustration and then relief

Dyed my hair purple

Spent £10,000 on American Express. £10,000 on Access. £1000 on Barclaycard

Very upset at first then thought sod it and went on a screwing rampage

Tried to be mature and adult about it. Called her new boyfriend names

Blamed myself completely. Immense guilt and remorse

HOW LONG DID IT TAKE BEFORE YOU FELT BETTER?

The batting of an eyelid

Never completely recovered

Six months then realized that I'd got to get on with my life

Six years. Well, I like a drama

DO YOU HAVE ANY ADVICE OR TIPS FOR THIS PHASE? HOW TO LET GO?

Don't get involved in the first place

Jump straight into another relationship (or several)

People change and not always together. Sometimes you just have to accept that and use a different bedroom

Learn to forgive yourself

Go to the movies a lot

Don't see them for a while if that's possible, especially don't try to rebuild any bridges you've already burnt. If you try to go back to make it 'OK', you'll end up getting burnt as well

Don't get lawyers involved if you can help it. They screw you, play you off against each other. They have you by the short and curlies and take most of the money. In fact our common hate of them almost reunited us. Almost

4

SEX, LIES AND SOLICITORS

> *For a while we pondered whether to take a vacation or get a divorce. We decided that a trip to Bermuda is over in two weeks but a divorce is something you can cherish forever*
>
> *Woody Allen*

Relationships, some you win, some you lose.

Lose a marriage, win a divorce. As Herb Caen said 'It is better to have loved and lost but only if you have a good lawyer.'

The Myth

That the only expense in getting divorced is the cost of the solicitor.

The Reality

Break open your piggy bank. You're going to need dosh and lots of it.

These days divorce is a marketable commodity. As well as the high cost of a solicitor, one or both of you are also going to need:

Don't even think about
trying to beat the system:

Day one

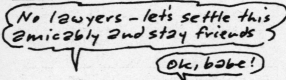

Day one hundred

A counsellor/therapist – that is if you want to keep some of your friends. Pay someone to listen to you and give your mates a day off

An estate agent – one of you's moving

> *She's a fine housekeeper. Every time she gets a divorce, she keeps the house*
> *Bob Hope about Zsa Zsa Gabor*

Add removal men, surveyors, property solicitors, decorators, workmen to connect gas, electricity, water, phone

Various new bits of furniture, appliances

Doctors – for valium, sleeping pills, tranquillizers

A good liquor store to supply you with lots of booze

The therapist again. This time to get you off the drink, drugs and seventeen-year-olds that you've now become addicted to

Various pamperers – for massage, facials, pedicures

Then there are the optional extras:

Private detectives – to have the ex followed

Social workers

An agent to sell your story to the gutter press

One man's pain is another man's gain.
    Next time you're hitching up with someone and you're having the 'we don't need two fridges, two TVs, two

beds, let's have a car-boot sale' conversation, wait. See if you can store it. If you don't need the stuff, I can guarantee one of your pals soon will.

A FEW INTERESTING FACTS ABOUT DIVORCE IN THE UK

(Well I thought so anyway.)

Women initiate seventy-three per cent of cases

There has been a fifty-four per cent increase in the divorce rate since 1980

100,000 divorces go through a year

In London, 1994, the average fee per hour for a divorce solicitor was £120

One in three modern marriages end in divorce

Divorce lawyers are at their busiest around New Year, after the joys of family Christmases and September, after the joys of summer holidays. According to the statistics, these periods are make or break

You can get a DIY divorce pack for £9.99 at WH Smith

Surveys of divorcees reveal that a significant proportion wish that they had never got divorced

> 'The chief cause of all divorces is matrimony.'

Mrs Lottie Myrons was granted a divorce when she told the judge that since their marriage, her husband had spoken to her three times. She was awarded custody of their three children

Readers Digest

LAWYERS

> "Nowadays a thoughtful girl saves a piece of her wedding cake for her divorce lawyer.'

Lawyers only deal with the financial and legal side, NOT the emotional. Before you talk to a lawyer, talk to a friend or counsellor, even the milkman, anyone who doesn't charge by the hour for you to get it off your chest.

They can take you through the process (Petition. Acknowledgement. Apply for decree nisi and prepare affidavit. Apply for a decree absolute), and see that the legal paperwork is done correctly.

They sort out finances and assets, who gets what and try their best to make sure arrangements between you, your ex and your kids are OK.

They explain the grounds and your rights. The way divorce is cited, one of you is the petitioner, the other the respondent.

> *A Bermudian wife, in seeking a divorce, insisted to the magistrate that her grounds for divorce were simple and sufficient. 'I have reason to believe that my husband is not the father of my child'*
>
> James Thurber

The Grounds for Divorce are:

- Adultery
- Unreasonable behaviour – drink, drugs, gambling, violence, extravagance, meanness, neglect, refusing to have sex or children, excessive sexual demand, mental instability, homosexuality, persistent nagging
- Two-year desertion
- Two-year separation with consent from respondent
- Five-year separation

Legal fees can be horrendous – the fight may cost more than it's worth.

Check charges per hour all the way down the line. It may surprise you what they charge you for. My friend Pete was talking to his lawyer and told him he would find some information pertinent to his case in that morning's paper. The solicitor went and bought the paper then charged him for the time it took him to walk to the paper shop and back, plus of course, the cost of the paper. At £200 per hour, it cost Pete £100.25. He could have posted him a copy for twenty-five pence. A barrister friend of mine told me of a case he'd recently read about where a client took her lawyer out to the opera (where she had first class seats) then on for an expensive dinner. Both were her treat, but later she found he had charged her for his time. Watch out for this kind of thing.

If you can settle out of court it will be much, much cheaper.

You may have to divulge very personal and intimate details to your lawyer so it's very important to find one you like and feel comfortable with.

Decide if you want a fighter or a conciliator. This, of course, depends on your relationship and what you want the outcome to be.

Sometimes even the lawyers fall out with each other. When my friend John was getting divorced there was a temporary hiccup when his and her lawyers refused to speak to each other.

> *The difference between a divorce and a legal separation is that a legal separation gives a man time to hide his money*
> *Attrib Johnny Carson*

ALIMONY

> *Alimony. Bounty after the mutiny*
> *Max Kaufman*

There are two ways to avoid alimony. Stay single or stay married, otherwise it's pay-up time – the screwing you get for the screwing you got. If you're on the paying out end it can feel, as Arthur Baer said, 'like buying oats for a dead horse'. But don't worry – if you don't pay alimony one month, your partner can't repossess you.

This is how it was for some of the divorcees I spoke to:

WAS THE SPLIT AMICABLE?

She said

No. He kept the guilt. I kept the rest

No, I'd like to have torn his liver out and fed it to the vultures

Is Bosnia peaceful?

He said

Yes. She got everything she wanted

Yes for me, no for her

Yes. We both hated each other

About as amicable as the raid on Pearl Harbor

HOW DID YOU DECIDE WHO KEPT WHAT?

He said

She'd already labelled what she wanted in anticipation

She got everything but it was worth it

I kept whatever was in easy reach through the window that I had to break

She said

I kept everything except his girlfriend

He moved abroad and took everything with him except for a silver hip flask. I gave that to Oxfam

Anything he could unscrew, he took, even the toilet seat, light bulbs, our daughters' toys. Then he went out in the garden and dragged a tree trunk in so that at least I had something to sit on. I suppose he thought that was funny

CHILDREN

> *The real killer is when you married the wrong person but had the right kids*
> *Ann Beattie*

Most kids'd prefer parents to stay together no matter how unhappy (unless the parent is violent). They can be depressed because they haven't got the power to stop what's happening.

A common kid's fantasy is that the parents'll get back together. If it's not on the cards, let them know, otherwise they may be disappointed when you don't.

Don't use kids unhappiness to punish your ex (by denying access) or turn kids against the ex.

Children need:

- To feel free to love both parents
- To know as much as possible about what's happening. Don't spring it on them
- Reassurance that it's not their fault
- Practical assurances – where they're going to live, go to school, how often they'll see both parents

I don't see Dad much any more, but I've got lots of nice new uncles!

- To know someone will always be there for security. They can think because one parent can go, so can the other

If one of you has a new partner, in the early days especially, kids still need time alone with you. Time that is theirs so that they feel that they matter too.

SOME 'DO'S AND DON'TS' FOR HANDLING THE KIDS

Don't

Criticise your ex

Disappear altogether

Hide all your feelings. Open displays are OK sometimes but full range ones can be a bit scary. Let them know you feel bad but not the details, tell these to your counsellor or friends

Discuss maintenance when the kids are around

Cross-examine them on their return

Make comments about new partner

Make them feel responsible for you or they can feel betrayed when you find a new partner

Pick on a child if they remind you of your ex or if one of your children lines up with the other side

Drop discipline because of exhaustion or fear of alienation

Buy their affection

Encourage them to defy their other parent

Introduce new partners in early visits, give them time

Do

Discuss changes in finances and lifestyle with them

Decide rules together. It's surprising how strict kids can be

Investigate if they seem reluctant to see your ex

Make yourself scarce or have a friend over when your partner comes to pick up the children if seeing each other is painful

Keep communicating. Others can help – family, friends, school, professionals – those uninvolved emotionally

Involve kids in planning access visits as they have lives (social, extra curricula) as well

Whatever the outcome, the whole process can leave you feeling drained, financially, emotionally and physically, so it's time to look at the next chapter, cures for a broken heart.

PART 2

GETTING OVER THE HUMP

5

CURES FOR A BROKEN HEART

> *Is there any cure for a broken heart? Only time can heal a broken heart, just as only time will heal his broken arms and legs*
> *Miss Piggy*, Miss Piggy's Guide to Life

It's early days, you probably feel horrible and tell people you wish they'd known you when you were alive. Forget about being nice, keeping it all together, give yourself a break.

HOW TO GET THROUGH THE EARLY DAYS

Do

Shun all sensible advice

Live on Ben & Jerry's Chunkie Monkey ice-cream, chips and toast

Only shop for food in expensive Italian delicatessens (I told you getting divorced was going to cost)

Take up smoking expensive French cigarettes, chewing tobacco, puffing on cigars

Think twice before accepting invitations to weddings. You

may get an uncontrollable urge to stand up and shout 'bollocks' at what should be a meaningful and affectionate moment for the couple

Dress like a slut and behave like a trollop at a dinner party set up by well-meaning friends to introduce you to their only single friend, who has acne and a dirty neck

Sit at street cafés drinking triple espressos and glowering at passers-by who look remotely in love or happy

Make divorce work for you. Develop the person of mystery image. You are a person with a past. Think glamour, you are a survivor and the story's not over yet. You have lived. Look the part. Dress only in black and it's probably a good idea to wear dark glasses – as some days, more than others, the fact you've had a past will show by the bags under your bloodshot eyes

Buy yourself one fabulously expensive outfit that makes you feel like a million dollars. Charge it to your ex

Avoid friends who believe in counselling and hang out with the bitchy friends who you dropped because your ex didn't like them and vice versa. Friends who say things like Dorothy Parker when she said, 'To me, Edith looks like something that would eat its young'. Let them verbally crucify your ex, blame him for everything and inspire you with inventive methods of revenge (as well as explaining how to charge the new outfit to him). Join in with some shockers of your own. Don't try to be nice, understanding or show any remorse or regret. You're not ready. If you do remarry, you'll probably take up 'nice' again then. For now, give yourself a break

Be horribly selfish and practise not feeling guilty afterwards. Guilt is a waste of time. (Don't feel even guiltier if you can't do this)

Go to the movies on your own in the afternoon

Drink so much you can hear the peanuts splash. Try whacky cocktails with filthy sounding names, they will keep up your spirits. If it feels as though your whole world has come to a standstill, you'll soon feel as though the world's revolving round again . . . and again . . . but this time it's booze not love

Watch shallow rubbish on TV and low-life films such as *Gilly goes to the Dentist for a Fillin' and a Drillin'*, *Rambo and his Naked Gun* and *Emmanuelle goes to Lourdes*

Don't watch anything with love in the title, especially avoid films like *Love Story* with shout-lines like 'love is never having to say you're sorry'. In actual fact, it's divorce that means never having to say you're sorry

Forget about books like *Women Who Ate Too Much, The Shite Report, Daft Women, Dafter Titles*. Although it's true to say that they're not books to be tossed aside lightly – they should be thrown aside with great force

Flick through *Hello* and try to figure out who's next for the chop out of this week's crop of horribly happily marrieds

Forget about cleaning your house. Send any washing out to the laundry

Stay away from gas ovens, high bridges, sharp implements and open windows

And finally, but most importantly, find some gorgeous horny young thing who is fascinated by your 'mystery

person with a past' image and get laid as often as possible in as many strange positions as you can still manage without bursting an artery.

NB: bit of sensible advice here:
don't forget the condoms but
do get the big boy, ribbed, hashish flavoured variety

Don't

Worry about the overdraft you have run up by accomplishing all of the above

Feel guilty about all of the above or in fact anything

Listen to friends who can see both sides of the divorce and aren't totally on your side

Listen to people who say anything remotely like, 'Hey, you may be in the gutter but you can still see the stars.' Or 'You'll get over it in time.' They are right but who wants to hang out with people who are always right? Isn't that why you left your ex? Wasn't he/she always right? For the time being, tell anyone who's right to bugger off and be quick about it

Look for a new interest to take your mind off things. When this nightmare phase has ended (and it will) you will be unable to make origami fish mobiles, tap dance or speak 'holiday German' ever again as long as you live

Try to be understanding

Think about sharing the blame

Worry about the future for at least three weeks

Try to have a meaningful relationship

Eat sensibly

Give up coffee, cigarettes or alcohol or impose any discipline on yourself

Try to have a good night's sleep

Go anywhere or do anything

You'll be ready to move on and be all understanding at some later stage, when you can really accept the situation and the scars have mended a bit, but for now you've got to lick your wounds a little. So go avoidance, go escapism, go oblivion. That's what it's all there for.

As for every nettle there's a dock leaf, so for every divorce there's a bottle of Mexican tequila and a copy of Jilly Cooper's *Riders*.

So you can't cope for a while, so you're full of venom and hate and nastiness. So you're a flawed human being. My favourite kind. Just look at high priests and priestesses of relationships. Think, do *I* want to be a smarmy self-righteous know-it-all who bakes their own organic bread with one hand, makes foreplay into a healing act with the other and *always* communicates (with sensitivity) before minor resentment becomes major confrontation? I don't think so.

Where would be the fun of making mistakes and falling flat on your face? There's no harm in falling or even lying there for a while until *you* feel like getting up, not when anybody else thinks you should. Stuff 'em. There's no time limit on your recovery. And talking of which . . .

IN TIME

> *Time may be a great healer but it's a lousy beautician.*

The heartache will pass. Time is the great healer but it can't half feel like he's a slow bugger when he's got a job like this to do. But it will pass. You may be dreading tomorrow, but think about it this way, in two days, tomorrow will be yesterday and you're already on your way to this thing being history.

If it feels like time is standing still for you, throw the clock out of the window and you'll soon see time fly.

In the meantime, here's a few words from my friends 'the divorcees'.

What cures can you recommend for a broken heart?

Join a rock 'n' roll band, go on a world tour

An eighteen-year-old model

Go shopping

Get laid as often as possible

Look at all the friends and good things you still have in your life. Don't go into denial. Have a good cry and enjoy it. Then go and buy a bottle of Bollinger, sit in the sun and get smashed with your best friend who's also been there, got the T-shirt

Only one cure – love

Meditate

Say yes to things you haven't done before

Get a Jessica Rabbit vibrator

A visit to see Eddie Izzard in stand-up

Lots of parties

Time, therapy

Death, a whiskey distillery or a lifetime's supply of valium

Indulge yourself on every level. Start by buying a new wardrobe

So there you have it from the pros.

6

SELF-HELP

> *My wife knew all about self-help, she*
> *helped herself to everything I had,*
> *including my pension*

What self-help isn't

Going round to your ex's when they're out and helping
yourself to whatever you can get into the back of the car.

What it is

When you're ready, you give yourself some time and space to
have a look at the emotional damage, do a bit of mending,
restore your confidence and maybe even discover why the
marriage went wrong in the first place. This can be valuable
because it can help you not to make the same mistakes again.

And how do you know when you're ready to take this
inner journey? You're ready when you can:

- Look at your wedding album without wanting to
  throw up
- Speak about your ex without wanting to do
  grievous bodily harm
- Think about starting a new chapter in your life as

opposed to just getting through the end of the
last one in one piece

It can be a confronting and difficult transition and you
may have to face uncomfortable and disconcerting revela-
tions about yourself and your part in the break-up. This is
why some divorcees choose never to look closely at what
happened and just plunge blindly into the next relationship
and hope that this time it works out.

However, it's only when you stop loading all the
blame onto your ex and take a percentage yourself, that you
can come out of the tunnel into the light and not into an
oncoming train.

As it is a sensitive time when your worst vulner-
abilities may feel exposed, you may need some support and
encouragement that you're not in it alone.

It can be a horribly confusing time, you don't know
who you are anymore or even what you think, it keeps
changing so often.

Times when:

- You feel your inferiority complex doesn't
  compare with others
- You can't make up your mind whether you're a
  repressed axe murderer or you want to be a nun
- Some days you think you may be gay, other days
  you think you might be a teapot
- You feel that even your analyst doesn't
  understand you
- You're not sure if admitting you need help is part
  of the solution, part of the problem, the solution
  to the problem or a separate problem altogether.
  You feel like Confucius when he say: 'who say I
  say all those things they say I say?'

- You're in two minds as to whether you're schizophrenic
- You feel that although you've overcome your paranoia, now everyone's jealous of you
- You're depressed about taking anti-depressants
- You drink to forget you're drinking too much
- You take drugs to escape the fact that you're taking drugs
- You're anxious that your next anxiety attack is going to be the mother of all anxiety attacks
- Becoming angry makes you furious
- Your counsellor told you that letting anger out was a healing thing and to pretend that she was your ex and let all the frustration out on her, you did. Your court case is on Wednesday. The song, 'you'll never walk alone' that you, she and the 'men as victims' help group sang when you were all sad has now been changed to 'she'll never walk again'
- You went to an assertion day but didn't dare go in
- You went to an 'asserting the new you' day but left because the registration form asked you to tick which you were: schizophrenic, mildly neurotic, borderline psychotic, anal compulsive, obsessive compulsive or just plain hysterical. You had already ticked all of them when you saw it said to tick *one* of the above
- Your supply of 'personal growth' books has grown all over the house
- Every weekend til Christmas is booked on a mind-expanding workshop and your old friends are getting worried
- Your doctor said no more pills, they're habit-

forming. You disagreed, arguing that you'd been taking them for ten years and never had a problem

- You don't want to go to therapy any more, the therapist was asking too many personal questions
- You were confused when your analyst charged you double because of your split personality. Part of you was happy to pay but the other part objected
- You decided to stop therapy because you don't trust a man with a couch in his office
- You went for help because you were feeling slightly cracked but now you're completely broke

Divorce is high on the stress scale, along with moving house. The chances are that you hit the jackpot and got to do both. Whatever your reaction, whether to run wild talking to anyone who'll listen, or withdraw and suffer in silence, the whole experience has probably left you feeling empty and drained, even if it's only financially.

In the early days of post break-up, friends and family are usually there being supportive, willing to lend a listening ear. Then comes a time you may feel they've had enough or maybe you've had enough and you want to move on, feel you *should* have moved on. You don't want to feel as if you're 'going on about it'. Trouble is, the length of time it takes to recover is different for everyone and if you impose a limit upon yourself saying, 'OK it's time I was over this by now,' the chances are you're only going to get more distressed because you're not over it. There's no harm in seeking a bit of help.

Trouble is where do you go, what do you do? You can go to the doctor and say I've got a broken leg or a boil on my bum and he'll give you a bandage or some ointment. But what can he give you for a broken heart, crushed confidence, shattered self-esteem? Camomile lotion and a course of antibiotics? If only.

Because the damage is unseen, except maybe for bags under the eyes and a few new wrinkles, it doesn't mean that it isn't there and just as painful as physical hurt. It's always best to recognize the symptoms, pay them attention and do whatever you can by way of remedy.

> *There's nothing wrong with a person's sex life that the right psychoanalyst can't exaggerate*
>
> *G.H. Bath*

There are some excellent counsellors out there and some excellent support groups who can provide what you need. And they can help you not only get over feeling blue but also understand what went wrong. Was your relationship stuck in a destructive pattern? Here's a few you might recognize.

Dependency

'You need me, I will look after you.' The rescuer and rescued.

Advantage: One of you gets looked after for a while, the other gets to play John Wayne or Mother Theresa.
Disadvantage: You owe, you pay.

Master/slave

'What I say goes – you just have to live with it.'

One partner gives in to the other who is always bossy and expects to get their way. OK, maybe he learnt that it's a dog-eat-dog world and if he doesn't dominate, he will be dominated. He was bullied at school, he's now the bully. The weak one usually has low self-esteem.

Advantage: One of you gets their way.
Disadvantage: The other resents it like hell, stores it up and doesn't say anything but gets acute arthritis in their early forties.

Smothering

'We are everything to each other.'

Advantage: Great in the beginning.
Disadvantage: Suffocation. Later when one partner needs space, it can be seen as a threat so they repress it. They daren't show any part of them that differs from the norm and any small move towards independence is seen as disloyalty. Often one sees the relationship as suffocating.

I love who I think you are

'You are perfect, you can't do anything wrong.'

One partner on a pedestal, the other blind to their faults and blaming themselves for any problems. The one on the pedestal stays in control by being distant. If they were more open, the other'd see their faults.

Advantage: One gets to be king of the castle and adored.
Disadvantage: They daren't ever come down and be real. It'd break the illusion.

Martyr

'Look how I suffer to make you happy.'

One partner says there's nothing they won't do for the other but martyrdom actually makes the other feel guilty. They can't be happy around someone who's so unhappy.

Advantage: One gets to control.
Disadvantage: Not a barrel of laughs as the one who is 'sacrificing' is actually very manipulative.

> *You can always tell the person who lives for others by the haunted look on the faces of the others*
>
> Katherine Whitehorn

Blasé

'If it's going to work it will – if not, too bad.'

They don't want to need anyone, can't handle problems and are scared to show vulnerability.

Advantage: Avoids all confrontation.
Disadvantage: For better and worse is OK as long as it never does get worse, in which case they're out of the door.

Polite Lodgers

'If we don't say anything, it'll be OK.'

Back to back with no communication. Like lodgers together, they live separate lives.

Advantage: No arguments.

Disadvantage: No nothing.

'Did you miss me while I was gone?'
'Were you gone?'

Healthy

They stand alone, independent, no leaning on or tangling or stepping on. Rare birds. Also a real pain to spend time with because they're usually so smarmy and pleased with themselves that they got it right.

Counsellors usually look at the three main blocks for a good relationship: communication, expectations and sex. They try to understand what went wrong, what happened.

- What attracted you in the first place?
- Why did it work when it did?
- What led to the failure?
- Is success in love based on a particular pattern?
- What if this changes?

Relate have an excellent team of trained counsellors who can help you look into this sort of area, they also help in your relationship with your children and if you're a bit broke they are flexible about fees, preferring you to come for help than to stay away because you can't afford it. At which point, I'd like to issue a Government Wealth Warning.

BEWARE the psychobabble hookers who tout for business with a line tailormade for the vulnerable. You have a need, a weakness, they have the product. But you'll pay for it. Your pain is their gain and they've bought the franchise.

'What becomes of the broken hearted?' Too many of them end up hooked to weekend workshops where the only way forward is another weekend at another £400.

These weekends are run by dubious ex-businessmen and women who see grief and lack of esteem as a market commodity. Sincerity is their job. Their names are Chip and Crystal or Chuck, which is appropriate because they make you want to do just that. They hug a lot and charge you £60 an hour to learn how to breathe. But you're desperate, they seem to understand and tell you 'THIS can make the difference. What have you got to lose?'

The next three month's pay cheque, that's what. They say they want to help, it's their life's mission, but if they want to help so much why don't they lower their prices?

Then there's the silent. They don't *hug*. They don't counsel or advise. They ask a few questions then interrupt and say 'and how do you feel about that?' You're confused, how the hell do you know what you feel about anything?

That's why you went to them in the first place. You have to sit in agonizing silence searching mind, heart and soul, desperately trying to come up with what it could possibly be that you *really* feel while they stare at you with, as Richard Gordon put it, 'the eye and warmth of a dead trout'.

At £40 an hour you could have bought a book on psychotherapy and a bottle of Cristal to down with a pal.

Understanding the destructive patterns of your last relationship can help you not to make the same mistakes again but don't expect miracles, self-help can't make your life perfect, it has its limits. Here's what the divorcees think.

What do you think about therapy and self help groups?

Crap

Great place to meet people. Everyone's busy bearing their souls so you know if you're in with a chance with them after an hour instead of after ten years

I prefer friends and alcohol

Useful up to a point, like in the acute stages of pain, not so helpful when you're more together

Sometimes they can nudge you out of a rut then it's up to you

The very time you need them is often the time you can't afford them or you have to wait six months to be seen

Therapy's OK but ditch the self-help group and all those well meaning Janes and Nigels

Ice-cream is better

I did find it useful to use lots of gratuitous bad language and jump up and down on my wedding photos. That's a therapy of sorts, I suppose

What sort of pattern do you feel you fell into in your relationships?

I'm good for six months then I introduce them to my underwear

Business folded lost my dosh. Divorce

Passion, cool down, go through the motions

Always choosing women who can't trust me. Then I prove them right

I start off with the 'let's be equal' pattern then think f**k this, I wanna be boss. My way or no way

Him Tarzan, me stupid

Not really communicating when the going got tough

Wendy and Peter Pan

Do you believe you can create what you want?

No, a ridiculous idea

Yes. There is no doubt about this

No. Raquel Welch is still living in Hollywood

Yes if you're rich enough

Yes. It worked for Henry VIII

With enough DNA and a robust laboratory, yes

Only if your fantasy is chocolate chip cookies

Yes, in everything except relationships

Fuck knows

7

THE JOY OF BEING SINGLE

> *Bigamy is having one husband too many.*
> *Monogamy is the same*
>
> *Erica Jong*

You may have discovered the cure for cancer, found out what happened in the Bermuda Triangle and negotiated a million-dollar book deal but there will *still* be those friends and family whose reaction will be to say, 'That's nice dear. And when are you going to settle down again?'

It's as though happiness doesn't exist outside couple-dom and yet some of the most fulfilled people I know are single and content to be so. Not one of them resembles Glen Close in *Fatal Attraction* with a penchant for boiling rabbits, nor are they like Miss Haversham, covered in cobwebs, sad, embittered and neglected. Single doesn't mean abandoned, past the sell-by date, emotionally imbalanced or desperate.

Alone needn't mean lonely, in fact it's much lonelier to be in a dead relationship than it is to be single. As John Mortimer said, 'Marriage is like pleading guilty to an indefinite sentence. Without parole.' You've just escaped, think about the choices now available!

The best thing about being single again is having some sex at last

> *I feel like a million tonight but one at a time*
>
> Mae West

Probably no one knows better than a divorcee just how much of a myth 'happily ever after' is. We're all fed it, the cornflakes family. Him, her, the kids, the dog, cat and the cornflakes breakfasts in large sunny kitchens with gardens in bloom behind. It's one of the myths that misleads many of us for great parts of our lives. That marriage makes you happy, having kids makes you happy, having a home makes you happy. Nothing is forever or has any guarantees.

As a single, the myth of happily ever after with a perfect partner may seem real again. It may feel that it was just that the last partner was the wrong one. Don't fall for it, rather enjoy some time alone.

You may feel lonely, but remember the time when you felt you had no space or privacy.

Maybe you don't like meals for one but remember when you always had to cook what your ex wanted or always had to eat at their favourite restaurant.

You may miss sex now, didn't you when you were married?

You may feel that you have no one to talk to now but remember when the ex looked up from his paper and asked if you said something and you replied, 'Yes, I did, last week.'

For the first time in years, you have the freedom of choice. Relish it, you may find you don't want to lose it again in the confines of another 'serious' relationship and all the compromise and bargaining that has to be done when you first meet.

ADVANTAGES OF A DIVORCEE

Driving

A whole new experience. You haven't got that irate passenger with the map sitting next to you saying, 'You should have taken that turn-off back there.' 'I told you so.' 'OK, OK, read the bloody thing yourself.'

Decorating

You want comfy old antiques? You can have them. You can redecorate to your taste. No more mixed interiors to accommodate his 'n' hers, no more Zen minimalist meets Russian opulence and looks like what it is – a compromise.

Telly

Worth the whole damn divorce. Sole use of the channel changer, you can flick and change to your heart's content. No one there to say, 'I don't believe you're watching this rubbish. Turn over, there's something more worthwhile on BBC 2!'

Three a.m., you can't sleep? Catch up with the latest in appalling soaps, there's no one there to complain.

Don't you feel strange being in this big house all on your own?

No Darling, 'cos now it's MY big house

Sleeping

You can sleep diagonally, sideways, upside-down, with your head under the pillow and bum in the air AND you get all the duvet and there's no twitching, snoring or squirming about to disturb you. And you can switch the light on to read.

Shopping

No more hiding stuff in the car boot or the back of the cupboard only to say, 'What, this old thing? I've had it years,' when you wear it. It's your money, you don't have to divide the price by three to make it sound acceptable to yourself.

Family and Friends

You don't have to worry about whose family to go to at Christmas, no mother-in-law, you can have all the friends your ex banned from the house back without worrying if she is bored or threatened or insulted.

Domestic

You can eat when you want, launder when you wish and you can leave the loo seat permanently up or down.

Social

You don't have to worry about your partner being unfaithful and you can use your ex and kids as excuses to get out of almost anything.

Looks

You don't have to keep shaving your chin or your legs.

Choice

You can do what you want, spend what you like.

Experiment, find out what you like after all this time. The world's your oyster. Discover new restaurants, find new friends, go to the theatre, exercise, take a lodger. There are no restrictions. No one is there to impose their view, opinion or preference. You're free. Rediscover life and all it has to offer. If shopping in the past has meant Asda, Safeways and Sainsbury's, break out. Save up and go to Paris with a friend. Do a Shirley Valentine or Stanley Valentine.

> *I don't want to see any faces at this party I haven't sat on*
>
> *Bonnie Raitt*

Tips

- Learn to be happy as a single person. If in doubt, spend a couple of days with anyone married more than five years
- Don't look for a marriage partner. Develop as many positive relationships as you can with both sexes
- Don't make someone else responsible for your happiness and passion. It's up to you

PART 3

HAPPY ENDINGS

8

STARTING AGAIN

> *Now I am beginning to live a little and*
> *feel less like a sick oyster at low tide*
> *Louisa May Alcott,* Little Women

OK, the self-abuse is over, no matter how much you enjoyed it.

You had enough of a go as tragedy queen or rejected hero.

It's time to move on (but you can go back to the bad ways suggested in Chapter Four on alternate weekends and Holy Days).

It's time to think about starting again.

First of all, get philosophical. Pick your ten favourite clichés and pin them on your wall (or your ex's forehead). These are going to be your inspiration in times of adversity from now on. Here's a few to be going on with:

1) When life closes a door, it opens a window
2) The darkest hour is just before dawn
3) Every cloud has a silver lining
4) When life hands you a lemon, make lemonade
5) Life's not a rehearsal
6) No use worrying about life because no one gets out of it alive

7) You can't make a hit if you have no aim
8) Everything changes, usually for the better
9) Grant me the serenity to accept the things I cannot change, the courage to change the things I can and the wisdom to know the difference
10) The years teach much which the days never know

Now you may still be feeling a bit fragile, feeling sorry for yourself like the only break you ever got was a coffee break, the only kick you got out of life was a kick in the teeth. Nothing goes right for you, you're the sort of person for whom nothing ever works, even your sun dial's slow, it rains when you have no umbrella, even the plastic flowers fade, you lose at solitaire, your only hobby's collecting dust.

This is a condition. It's called depression, it distorts and disguises everything and it's time to knock it on the head.

Get rid of negativity and focus on the positive.

You're not the only person who married for life then discovered your partner didn't have any.

Now you've got another chance. A new chapter where you can create the kind of life you really want. In order to do this, it's a good idea to really think about what it is you want.

Set yourself goals, short- and long-term. Think about what you'd want from a new partner if you were to meet anyone. Go for what you want rather than just drifting into whatever comes your way. Make things happen.

Don't believe that only another person can make you happy. Look after yourself. You can't control your ex but you can control what you do to your body: diet, treats, rest, exercise, relaxation.

Let your anger out in a physical way: squash, tennis, gardening.

Eat well. Take Vitamin B for stress. If you eat rubbish, you will lose the stamina you need to cope with stress and it's a downward spiral.

Learn to meditate, it's calming and will help with panicky feelings.

Symbolize the new start, buy a new bed. Rearrange the furniture.

Treat yourself, don't wait for what your ex would have done and feel sorry for yourself. Go to Florence for the weekend with a friend. Find out what gives you pleasure.

Dare yourself to do the things you've always dreamed about. Allow for set backs and days when you feel that nothing has changed and even the old relationship looks good.

REWRITING THE SCRIPT

Until now your focus has most likely been on the past, what happened, memories and getting through the present. Life seems more like survival than fun. Any thoughts of the future may seem bleak but now's the time to take control. You choose and at this point you can either sink or swim. It may mean breaking old patterns of behaviour, moving on and making new friends.

Take it a step at a time, trying to accomplish total change and success all in one go can lead to a feeling of defeat if it doesn't happen. The best way is to set yourself minor goals within the major plan.

This is also the time you can start to rediscover yourself and what you want on every level. Do you prefer Douwe Egberts coffee but always bought Kenco because that's what he liked? Do you like the radio on in the morning but never listened because she objected? Rediscover the real you.

This time is a new start not an end, an opportunity to rewrite the script, why not give yourself the lead role? Think movies.

You're the writer and the director. If you don't want someone on the set anymore, they're dull, boring and their lines are awful. Out they go.

Who else would you like to star in your film? You get to cast it too. Tall, dark, blonde, young, old? Find them, they're out there somewhere. Think about what kind of relationship you want or what kind of friend you always wanted, toy boys, good time girls, the sincere, the supportive, the enthusiastic, the fun. Go get 'em. There's nobody saying 'Where are you going?' 'Where've you been til this hour?' 'Who with?'

THE CLOSED WORLD OF COUPLEDOM

Many of the divorcees I spoke to said until they were breaking up with their partners, they hadn't realized that most of their friends were couples.

Suddenly they were thirty-five years old and the only single and unattached on the block. Free at last to go out and party and all their mates were home reading *Postman Pat* to under-fives or tucked up with a cup of Horlicks and a good book.

Their diaries were empty and it wasn't just their ex that had deserted them.

1) Suddenly you're not Jane or Michael anymore, you're an 'odd number'. They don't want to

emphasize the fact that you're on your own so decide it's best to leave you out this time.

2) You may be a threat to their security – they might think they'd be better off single too, the other man's grass . . . They don't want their partner getting ideas from you.

3) You may be seen as a threat because you're available. The fact that you're still reeling and sex is the last thing on your mind, the only thing you can imagine laying is the dinner table, is beside the point. To some, you're single, you're available and you're not invited anymore.

4) And some folk just don't know how to deal with it, like with the bereaved. Rather than be faced with an awkward situation where they don't know what to say and fear you may be emotional and ruin their well-planned dinner party, they just simply avoid it happening by freezing you out.

Of course there are the old faithfuls who don't give a toss about any of the above and are wonderful throughout, but chances are they have partners and kids of their own and however much they do care, they still have their lives and responsibilities to get on with.

Get yourself some single friends. With the couples who don't know how to behave, see them one-to-one at first and tell them how you'd like to be treated and see how it goes, chances are you don't really want them as friends anymore anyway.

Your best bet is to seek out some friends who are either single or in the same boat. People who you can hang out with at weekends (always the worst time for the newly divorced). People you can call to go to the theatre and they don't have to get permission from their spouse or arrange a babysitter. People who love the fact that you're available, company, a new playmate.

9

THE DATING GAME

> *Burt Reynolds once asked me out. I was in his room*
>
> *Phyllis Diller*

The good news is that you may be single again, but you're no longer a spinster or a lonely bachelor.

You're a divorcee ... with a mysterious past. Remember?

OK so the only mystery is why you stayed so long in such a dead relationship. No one needs details.

The bad news is what comes next.

THE HORRIBLE TRUTH

According to certain philosophers and mystics, in life there are certain laws that cannot be changed, like gravity. This is one of them.

True love only comes when you've genuinely given up looking and are happy by yourself.

Of all the laws in life, this has to be the cruellest.

Where's the fun of getting what you want when you no longer want it? S'like wanting a Barbie doll when you're five, desperately, passionately, everyone else has got one. But do you get one? Yes, when you're eleven and have grown out of that phase.

How this law should really go is:

- When you're at your most desperate and don't know how you're going to make the mortgage payments, you'll win the pools
- When you've cried three nights minimum and feel that your life is empty and desolate, a fabulous looking man will appear at your door and offer to mow your lawn, take you out for dinner, make you laugh all night then introduce you to sexual paradise

But I suppose that, as my friend Greta would say, 'is too easy and not character-strengthening enough.'

So in recognition of this law . . .

Forget about joining bridge clubs, night classes, Saturday T'ai Chi and Club Med holidays in the hope you might find 'the one' (or should I rephrase that as 'the next one'?). All crap.

Only go ahead if you really want to study T'ai Chi or whatever, in which case, according to this theory, you'll probably meet the love of your life at registration.

WHERE DOES ANYONE MEET ANYONE NEW THESE DAYS?

At work, at a garden party, through friends, at the deli, out of the blue. When you're not looking and when you do meet them, they're not always what you expected.

Sadly no knight in shining armour is going to come

charging in to the rescue on a white horse like in the books. These days it's more likely his only means of transport will be a clapped-out Volvo and his gorgeous damsel is in distress because of her drink problem. Instead of riding off into the sunset together, they'll both be seen at AA.

'Hello. I'm the Lady of Shallot and I'm an alcoholic.'

The rule is – you want another partner, you've got to get yourself a life first. A life you're truly happy with, not put on to hide your feelings or numb the pain.

If you go out of your way to meet new partners to fill in a gap or 'make it right', it can be guaranteed that they're going to be unsuitable. I know because I've done it.

Once, when I was in between lovers (and I don't mean the five-in-a-bed fun kind of in between), I went out looking. In the company of two well-meaning friends, I did the round of fashionable wine bars, discos and clubs, places I'd never normally go. We flirted, we drank Kir Royales, we laughed loudly til the early hours.

And then I'd go home and want to slit my throat. I didn't fit in there so I thought I didn't fit in anywhere anymore. Just the thing you need when your confidence is six degrees below zero.

Still, if you're really stuck as to where to go to meet people, here's a few suggestions provided by well-meaning acquaintances:

King's Cross
Telephone kiosks
Work
Yellow pages
Through friends
Brothels
Railway arches
Sixth form college

Petrol stations
Supermarkets
Outside court
Sainsbury's, the Savoy, or anywhere in between
At AA, or AlAnon
Ads in *Time Out*
Night classes
Tennis clubs
Therapy groups
Everywhere

WHEN DOES ANYONE EVER MEET ANYONE OF VALUE?

When you've given up looking that's when. When you've finally adjusted to life on your own and you're happier than you've ever been. You're not even sure you'd want a partner now. You're at peace for the first time in years. Then guess what, along comes trouble.

Love always pops up when you least expect it. It's rotten like that but it's how it is. It arrives when you've given up looking and are finally getting on with life. Then along it comes, inconvenient as ever, and messes up your new-found tranquillity.

'Why didn't you come when I was lonely, needy, desperate?' you ask in fury.

Think about it.

Do you want a hopeless clingy emotional wreck with no life? No. Neither does anyone else. So don't try to manufacture love affairs until you're mended.

OK there may be a few strays along the way that in the illusion of the moment you may think is the next 'one'. It happened to my friend Annie . . .

Monday

I think I've met my soul-mate. I've never felt like this before, ever, even when I was first married.

Tuesday

I'm SO in love. I'd forgotten sex could be this good.

Wednesday

He didn't call today. I'm sure it's over, I must have said something wrong. He obviously thinks I'm too old and wrinkly. Oh God, my life is over. Maybe I'll leave another message on his answer machine, maybe he didn't get the first.

Thursday

Oh him? Nah. S'over. Got the 'let's be friends' line. We could have been so good together too. I'll never meet anyone like him again. I'm doomed to be alone for the rest of my life. I want to die.

Friday

Guess what? Last night the most inCREDIBLE thing happened. I've *really* met the one this time. I've never felt like this. What's that? I did on Monday. No that was different. This is the guy who is really going to change everything and make me happy.

And why not? These affairs do serve their purpose. They might see you through some bad nights and restore a bit of

confidence, remind you sex doesn't always have to be that same ole stroke, twiddle and grope you knew with your ex. Just don't get stuck on them, don't look for the meaningful one-night stand and *definitely* don't marry anyone in a hurry.

You've been married to one partner and it didn't work out.

Don't be too anxious to make another relationship work just to prove to yourself that you can or because you're on the rebound. There's a whole world of characters out there, each one would bring something different out in you and you in them.

So think about what you want next. Sample a few of the different flavours, play the field a bit before you start thinking about commitment and fidelity again.

Enjoy your freedom for a while, do all the things you've really wanted and if someone falls alongside. Fine. More than fine.

In the meantime, look at the choices:

Men

DIY man, boy scout camp leader, nice guy, prince, toy boy, diplomat, trainspotter, model maker, philosopher, academic, careerman, bookworm, writer, poet, visionary, romantic, dreamer, artist, new age man, svengali, mystic, hero, macho man, adventurer, warrior, chauvinist, athlete, mountain rambler, soldier, sailor, casanova, charmer, family man, King Whazza dick.

Women

Goodtime girl, flirt, princess, nympho, playmate, bimbo, career girl, harlot, one of the lads, free independent spirit, poser, intellectual, born-again virgin, earth mother, slave, feminist, madonna, innocent, searcher, healer, witch, mystic, saint, humanitarian, do-gooder.

Take your pick, they're all out there and many, many more. And when you've found someone you like the look of, it's time for a date!

First dates are bad enough when you're fifteen. They can be a complete nightmare when you've been out of circuit for a while. A grown up with one marriage behind you and going through all this again.

- What to wear?
- Where to go?
- Who pays these days? Are we equal or not? Does he pay, she pay, both pay or do you make a run for it after pudding?
- Do you go in for coffee? What does 'coffee' mean nowadays?
- And when do you bring up condoms, AIDS and

the fact you have five children, a dog and a budgie waiting for you to get home and report on how it went?

Don't give in and settle for a life in front of *EastEnders* because it seems the easier option.

By now you probably know what suits you. Wear what you feel good in.

Go somewhere you can talk, a restaurant for lunch or dinner rather than a theatre or cinema where you get the chance to know Tom Cruise or Julia Roberts intimately but are none the wiser about your date.

Test the ground to see who pays. A lot of men still like to pay, especially in the early days, and a lot of women are happy to let them do so. Offer to contribute and see what reaction you get. If you feel very strongly about it but the man wants to pay first time, let him and say 'but I'll pay next time'. There are so many mixed views on this subject that there are no longer any rules. Play it by ear.

You may have to relearn the art of small talk. You may have spent your last years discussing breastfeeding, nappies, the merits of *Jungle Book* versus *Pingu the Penguin* as a distraction for five-year-olds and now you're going out with a grown-up.

You may have spent the last years of your relationship learning to be honest with your ex, maybe tried Relate, to learn about true communication. Now forget it. It's not that you have to lie, just don't tell the whole truth.

Right

DATE: And how are you this evening?
YOU: Great thanks. I've been really looking forward to this evening. And how are you?

Wrong

DATE: And how are you this evening?

YOU: Terrible. Gimme a drink. And that's another thing I'm worried about. I'm drinking too much since the break-up. Oh I did tell you I just broke up with my wife didn't I? You know I still miss her and the kids. Life's a bitch and then I married one. But hey, you won't really understand unless I tell you the *Whole* story . . . it all started back in the days when we were both at college . . .

Keep it light, especially in the beginning.

LINES TO OMIT FROM FIRST DATE CHATS

- My analyst would like to meet you.
- I'm so horny, I haven't been laid in a decade and I intend to make up for lost time now.
- Can you cash me a cheque? My ex cleaned me out.
- I really want my next relationship to last forever.
- Do you believe a person can love more than two people at the same time?
- Do you mind if I cite you in my divorce?
- The next man I'm with has to really want a family and all it stands for, all the things I never had with Jim. I want real commitment this time.
- I don't want to waste time gameplaying. Either someone wants a relationship with me or not. SO?
- I'm forty, unemployable and very, very sad.
- My ex had an affair, I think she may have passed

on something nasty to me. I think it may be
herpes but I'm not sure. Do you know what the
symptoms are?

● I've been really enjoying my freedom and the
chance to sleep with so many different types of
people.

● I'm a single parent with five kids.

Some things you have to break to people
gradually and in small doses. For example:

January: The first date
February: 'This is Mark my 'eldest'
March: 'And this is his sister, Mary'
April: 'And her sister, Jane'
May: 'And my youngest, the twins Eddie and
Neddie'
June: 'And my mother lives with us . . . with her
cats'
July: 'And her mother'
August: 'And this is our social worker'
September: 'And this is Peter, Mark's probation
officer.'

A tip from the wonderful Ken Cambell which could be
adapted if you actually *want* to get rid of someone. He says, 'if
you're sitting on a train and some arse comes along and looks
at the empty seats around you then asks if anyone's sitting
there, reply, 'No. There's only me . . . And Jesus.'

That should shift them.

GOLDEN RULES

> *Don't let any guy put anything over ya,*
> *except an umbrella*
> Mae West

Don't pressurize

Don't be desperate:

Right

HE: Fancy a date?
SHE: Maybe.
HE: How about next week?
SHE: I'll let you know.

Wrong

HE: Hi. Fancy a date?
SHE Sure. When? I'm free tonight.
HE: I was thinking of next week.
SHE Why? What are you doing tonight?
HE: Well, I'm working.
SHE Oh I'll come over and cook for you then. I bet you
    don't eat right. I could help you with your work.
HE: But . . .
SHE What's the matter? You got someone else coming
    tonight? You don't really like me do you? . . . I'll
    change.
HE: But, but . . .
SHE Huh. Thanks for the enthusiasm. That's it. It's over.
HE: Ug . . .

Don't stay in, waiting for the phone to ring. One way to avoid this is, after meeting someone you like and they say, 'I'll give you a call' say, 'No I'm in and out such a lot, it's easier if I call you.' Let them stew instead

Don't be afraid to say no

Don't be too grateful

Don't rush in

Don't be too available

There was a young lady called Gloria
Who was had by Sir Gerald du Maurier
And then by six men
Sir Gerald again
And the band at the Waldorf Astoria

Don't go on about your ex

Don't date anyone who you used to baby-sit/teach or is a friend of one of your kids, i.e.: anyone who says things like 'awesome', 'brill', or 'magic' and has to be home by ten p.m.

Don't date anyone who three years ago you would have turned down saying I'd have to be desperate first and now even *they* are starting to look good. Wait a while

Don't take rejection too personally

And for you chaps? here's a page from an earlier version of this book, *How To Get Along With Girls* by Walter S. Keating (published 1944).

How not to offend
10 don'ts for the lover

1) Don't make her wait! If you cannot keep an engagement, telephone or send a wire. Or better, break a neck to get there. Waiting gives her that 'jilted' feeling which is not easily forgiven.
2) Don't find fault! You can get used to an outlandish hat or purple lipstick, you can get used to almost anything. But if you must make suggestions, be tactful. Use so much sugarcoating that the criticism will hardly show.
3) Don't have a roving eye! Nothing will upset her so much as your staring at another girl or making remarks about her legs.
4) Don't brag about your amours! Neither to her nor to anyone else. Heaven help you if you get the reputation of a man who 'kisses and tells'!
5) Don't be a wolf! A girl's casual smile is not an invitation to make passes. When she is ready for your kisses, she will give you a 'go-ahead' signal.
6) Don't make love in public! If you fail to see how ridiculous it looks, consider her feelings. The only public places where kissing is permissible are railway stations and boat docks.
7) Don't tell her you love her just to be nice! It is definitely not nice, it is a lowdown trick.
8) Don't tell questionable jokes! You will only embarrass her and give yourself a bad name.
9) Don't let a young girl take more than one drink! If she gets sick or slopped, you will both regret the night. She will not forgive you for having seen her at her worst.

10) Don't get slopped! If you cannot hold your liquor and you must have it, stick to the stag line.

Hah! Some things never change. Don't forget boys, don't let those young girls get too slopped.

And if you're wondering if what men and women want these days has changed since you were first out there, don't worry, everyone's just as confused as ever.

WHAT DO MEN WANT THESE DAYS?

Here's what my divorcee friends said.

He said

Men want to be understood without actually communicating to their partner what they are feeling

Tits that never sag, bums that never soften and a woman who is a mindreader, a whore and a Manchester United fan

To go back to the old days of harems and eunuchs

Money

Rude underwear, high heels, lotsa head, lotsa pussy, then back in the cupboard

A quiet life

No hassle. The worst thing that feminism did was create this fight about everything

Initially lots of sex and ultimately someone who makes them laugh a lot

Sex, long legs, blue eyes, sex, blonde hair, sex.

An intelligent, assertive yet somehow compliant and submissive mother-type who has an impressive career yet still finds time to cook and clean. Oh yeah, and big tits

Equal sex drives

A solid, reliable, honest woman

She said

An eighteen-year-old whose breasts point north who cooks like Floyd and fucks like a fireball. And then goes home

A mother

Women who are not afraid to be women

She may be 'she who must be obeyed' but *he* is 'he who must be understood'

Admiration, strength, kindness, great body, great brain, great lay

WHAT DO WOMEN WANT THESE DAYS?

He said

Solid, reliable, honest women

Money

A good social life, to be able to eat chocolate without getting fat, gossip and fulfilment

A good smack round the earhole

Someone to look after them (still)

Anything they can get away with

A big house, a Jaguar, two children, a Range Rover, an account at all major stores etc, etc. Same as always

I don't think they know

Commitment

To be considered better looking than Michele Pfieffer, even if they look like Dot Cotton.

To be men

A lover, housekeeper and a provider with no strings attached

She said

A heart of gold and a knob like a milk bottle

Buddha with balls and a Bentley

Everything – equal pay, equal say, exotic things done to them

Multiple orgasms – now

Tom Cruise with the care and compassion of Terry Waite

To be Mrs Kevin Costner

Someone who can make them laugh and pay the bills

Neil Pierson

Not to be patronized, to be respected and adored

Mel Gibson on toast

> *What women want, careers, friends, love*
> *and three-dollar pantyhose that won't run*
> *Phyllis Diller*

10

SEX AND SEDUCTION

> *There was a little girl*
> *Who had a little curl*
> *Right in the middle of her forehead,*
> *When she was good, she was very, very*
> *   good*
> *And when she was bad, she was very, very*
> *   popular*
>
> *Max Miller*

THE RULES OF SEDUCTION

1) *Turn the tables*

Stanley and Iris is a movie starring Robert de Niro and Jane Fonda as a couple who start off working together in a cake factory and eventually fall in love. There's a part in the beginning of the film where Stanley tells Iris that he's noticed that on her sad days, she wears her grey sweater, on her happier days she wears a pink one.

'You've been watching me,' she says accusingly.

'You stand out,' he replies.

Great line. And in that small scene you have the first rule of seduction. He turned the tables – it was her fault, she was irresistible, she couldn't blame him, she stood out.

Everyone likes to think they do, everyone tries to in their own way, so when someone notices the fact and declares it, you think, ha, smart and give them ten points straight away.

Most likely, part of the reason you split with your ex is because you no longer stood out for them, they took you for granted, part of the furniture, and the fact that you have beautiful eyes, a winning smile or a great sense of humour hadn't been acknowledged for years.

In order to seduce, you've got to go back to the first rule.

Make the seductee feel like the seducer, you're drawn in despite yourself. They are responsible, they stand out and you are just reacting like a moth to the flame.

2) *Always leave them wanting more*

You've clicked, you fancy this person like mad. You're laughing, the body language is comfortable. You're leaning in to each other. You feel like you could talk for hours. The chemistry's humming. Time to leave.

Probably the last thing you want to do but you can be sure they feel the same way too and will look forward to your next meeting.

3) *Forget chat-up lines*

Although I was always a sucker for the 'trust me I'm a doctor' line myself, generally chat-up lines or premeditated approaches tend to ruin any spontaneity and come across as crass.

4) *Temptation/resistance*

A hint of a promise. You're tempted but must resist. Go and see the play *Les Liaisons Dangereuse*. Essential viewing for anyone thinking about seduction. It's all about withheld passion, the torment of temptation and the sweet pain of an enormous passion which must be overcome.

It also helps if you're wearing something like the fab calf-length coat Alan Rickman wore in the version he starred in. You could tell it made him feel seductive just putting it on. The way he swished about in it, smouldering with desire and wickedness was very convincing. (I live in North London, Alan.)

Being seductive is always easier if you've got the right kit on. And then, when at your most beguiling, with signals emanating from every pore that say, 'I am the lay of the century. I am the one with whom you could find not only the G spot but the whole darn A to Z plus a whole new alphabet of spots in Hebrew, Greek and Arabic,' then you confuse the seductee with the message, 'but I'm trying to reform and mend my insatiable ways.'

An irresistible challenge to anyone to get you to change your mind.

5) *An element of the unattainable*

This leads on from number four really. People always want what they can't have. It's not exactly like playing hard to get, more like 'I'm not really available but ah, it's tempting'.

Reluctance up to the last minute when you give in to the heat of the moment works much better than 'I'm in the bedroom, come and get it'.

6) *Take it slow*

Don't sleep with new partners too soon. Think avocado. Ever tried eating one that isn't ripe yet? Exactly.

A look in the eyes, innuendo, body brushing, a hand on an arm briefly or brushing a hair off a shoulder can be more erotic and exciting than hours of sweaty, naked grinding and bouncing about.

I want a divorce!

7) *Encouragement/flattery*

There's no greater turn on than someone you fancy who is obviously turned on by you.

Forget the cool mask that says 'I've seen it all before' but thinks, 'I'm not going to let you know how aroused I am by you because I've been hurt and don't want to be again.'

Someone who is obviously aware of your sexuality and gets visibly cheerful when there's the slightest hint of ankle or come hither look in the eyes is much more fun than someone who hardly responds at all.

We all need encouragement, especially when past the age of twenty-five. The thing about having been with one partner for a while is you got used to each other's bodies and the way you were growing older together. Suddenly you're not young anymore and you have to take your clothes off in front of a new partner. Aaaaghhh. Chances are they're feeling the same so encourage each other. Though I did think Tom Conti as the Greek chappie in *Shirley Valentine* was going a bit far when he kissed her all over and told her that her stretch marks were beautiful. As she so rightly commented, 'Aren't men full of shit?'

The key to convincing flattery is to notice what is genuinely attractive and say so. A specific – eyes, mouth, hair, back teeth not just the general 'oh you're just gorgeous'. Most people know exactly what their best attributes are and so will know you're on the level if you flatter those in particular. *Then* you can go for the general.

Just a note here, if you are worried about a body that through time has taken the slow journey south, invest in some nice underwear (if you're female that is but whatever turns you on!) a good bottle of wine and some candles for flattering lighting for the over-twenty-fives. And for the day, get a girdle, a device that holds you in when you're going out.

8) *Ambiance*

Seduction is all about ambiance, atmosphere.

New York is romantic, Bognor Regis isn't, champagne is, lager isn't, roses are, a potted petunia isn't.

Creating an ambiance needn't mean expense necessarily but it does mean forethought and a little care. It's back to the 'you stand out' bit again, another way of saying you are worth some effort. But before you charge off and buy up the Barry Manilow soft songs CD, find out what romance means to your new lover and how they like it to be expressed. Some like the clichéd romance of champagne, hearts and roses. Others are more touched by practical acts of kindness, picking someone up from the station after work on a Friday night, bringing breakfast in bed. A good general clue, though, is appeal to all the five senses: lighting that is easy on the eye, music that is mellow and relaxing, scent that is fragrant, tastes that are tantalizing. Then you're ready for the last – touch.

9) *Have fun*

> *A voice from the vaseline jar.*
> *This too is love*
>
> *Gavin Ewart*

The sad thing about many long-term relationships is that the sex becomes routine, put on the Things to Do list.

Replace the hall light-bulb, clean the bathroom, phone bank manager, perform monthly bonk. A case so often of you knew, or at least thought you knew, your partner so well that you stopped making any effort.

'You put that there, I wriggle like this, you twiddle this, I twirl on that,' and it was over and time to do the school run.

With a new lover you can explore not only what they like but also discover some new things about yourself.

Sometimes though, experimenting with a new lover can be full of surprises. If only:

- You could find the key to the handcuffs
- She'd come back and untie you
- He hadn't brought the *whole* football team
- The neighbours don't suspect when they see the rope burns
- The rips in the car roof weren't so obvious
- She'd come and collect the German shepherd dog
- He'd tell you if you get to keep the boy scout
- You hadn't ended up in traction
- You knew a man who knew a man who repaired waterbeds
- Your children didn't object to the tattoos
- You hadn't run out of mayo/jelly/chocolate fudge/mangoes

Yeah. If only.

The sex experts have one tip about sex with a new partner. They say it's important to tell your lover what pleases you and vice versa but to do this in an encouraging way, not using negatives.

Right

'That feels really good and could you just nibble a bit there and . . . ooh, aah, aaay.'

The Stepford wives sort of had the right idea. You just have to add a bit at the end, 'You're the best. You're the Master . . . And could you just turn upside down for a moment? Whe-hey.'

Same applies if you're a chap. Most women I spoke to said they wouldn't object at all if a man used the same line, 'You're the best. You're the Master.'

Basically we all need a bit of encouragement.

Wrong

'For Christ's sake, stop going at me like you're rubbing a carpet stain. Don't you know ANYthing???? Do it like this.'

Exit new lover, stage left.

Some divorcees though, can't imagine ever having sex again, like my friend Marie. 'Sex?' she said, 'no thanks. I've had it all filled in and a gas fire fitted.'

No harm in waiting if you don't feel like it and if your new partner doesn't understand that you need time, bin the bastard.

Here's what the divorcees I spoke to said on the subject of sex.

WHEN YOU STARTED HAVING RELATIONSHIPS AND SEX AGAIN, DID YOU HAVE TO RELEARN ANY RULES?

He said

Not to say my ex's name when on the job

To refrain from farting in intimate moments

Lose a few pounds and remember to wear clean underwear

To make 'em laugh

Not to make out every cheque to my ex wife

She said

Not to be too eager to get undressed

Not to be too eager to please

Not to confuse contraceptive pills with hay fever tablets

To look for love, don't compromise

Not to panic and go with anyone

Relearning to be a real slut. It's an art that takes time

11

HAPPY ENDINGS

> *I don't for the life of me understand why*
> *people keep insisting marriage is doomed.*
> *All five of mine worked out*
>
> Peter de Vries

The main concern of most divorcees on finding a new partner is how to avoid making the same mistakes.

Don't worry, you won't. You'll make splendidly awful, brand new ones. Every partnership brings its own particular brand of defences, patterns and ways of dealing with the rough and the smooth. Nobody's perfect and there's no magic formula you can apply to avoid the inevitable roller-coaster of any love affair.

So take a deep breath, let the past be and take the plunge.

Don't let a marriage that went sour prevent you from having a good time now.

My friend Kate discovered that her suspicions about her husband cheating on her were correct. One of his girlfriends, sick of his lies (he wasn't even being faithful to his mistress) had blown his cover and confirmed what Kate'd thought all along.

When she confronted him with it he said: 'Well at least I've shown you what men are really like.'

Three years later and she's happily married to a wonderful, funny and faithful hunk.

'I wasn't about to let him ruin my life,' she said. 'He showed me what *he* was like, not all men.'

Some would say it was the triumph of optimism over experience but it worked for her.

I asked the divorcees I knew what they thought makes love work. Here's what they said.

WHAT IS THE SECRET OF A GOOD RELATIONSHIP?

He said

One where I'm living with Claudia Schiffer

Give and take

Humour. And money

God knows

Talking and laughing

A nun and a monk

Chemistry

Communication

Can't tell you. It's a secret

Seeing each other as little as possible

Psychotherapy before the wedding

She said

Being friends. You can have sex with anybody

A blind wife and a deaf husband

You tell me

Lesbianism

Laughing, sex, space, separate interests, respect, trust

Accepting your partner can't be responsible for your happiness

Love

WHAT WOULD YOU DO NOW IN A NEW RELATIONSHIP TO ENSURE YOU DON'T MAKE THE SAME MISTAKES?

He said

Listen, talk, administer regular beatings

Meet once a fortnight, or weekly at maximum

Check out the mother

Live with her on a desert island

Have separate bank accounts

Never have sex outside the relationship. Unless she says it's OK

Keep all my favourite art treasures and possessions in a rucksack by the front door

Talk things through if they weren't going well

Never get married again

She said

Have lunch with his ex wife

Have more respect for myself

Never accept vague excuses or evasive answers

Live separately and see them a few times a week

Try to compromise more and not be so demanding

Be more demanding and try not to compromise so much

DO YOU THINK GOOD RELATIONSHIPS JUST HAPPEN OR DO YOU MAKE THEM GOOD BY WORKING ON THEM?

He said

Fated. They just happen

They happen *then* you have to work on it. A Master in marine biology is child's play in comparison

They happen and then you make them bad by working on them

Just happen. If you have to work on them then something is fundamentally wrong

She said

You have to work at them

It's luck

You make them work by lying to yourself

Work like a dog

So, none the wiser there. All goes to show, different strokes for different folks an' all. Maybe the secret is to find someone who agrees with your answers to these questions.

For some it works to have the kind of traditional relationship where he is the breadwinner and she stays in the cupboard until it's time to come out for sex and supper. I know lots of couples that works for. Well OK, one. Others wouldn't stand for that, preferring a more equal partnership.

Whatever you want, before you get seriously involved, find out what it is you *both* want, is it the same? Find out if you share the same basic values – work, education, politics, religion. How do you feel about kids? Are you cat lovers or chasers? Is she a Sunday evening whip girl or choir mistress in church?

If you're still worried about love the second, third or whatever time round, here's few pointers to confuse you even more. Stick to these and you can't go wrong.

> *Oh life is a glorious cycle of song*
> *A medley of extemporanea*
> *And love is a thing that can never go*
> *wrong*
> *And I am Marie of Roumania*
> > *Dorothy Parker*

R is for respect and realistic expectations. Blessed is he who has none for he is not disappointed. Nobody can satisfy another on every level, every day unless of course they're very, very rich, in which case it's a lot easier.

> *I'd marry again if I found a man who had £15 million and would sign over half of it to me before the marriage and guarantee he'd be dead within a year*
> *Bette Davis*

E for effort. Don't let the rot set in.

L for laughter. Couples who can laugh together often stay together and the man who says his wife can't take a joke has usually forgotten himself.

A for acknowledgement, appreciation. Letting each other know you still find each other attractive is an important part of keeping love alive and so easy to let slip after the initial get together.

Right
Tell him he looks like the beginning of spring when in fact you mean he looks like the end of a hard winter.

Wrong
HER: I've just come from the beauty parlour
HIM: Too bad they were closed

When she's worried about aging and asks if you think she'll lose her looks as she gets older, don't reply if only you are that lucky.

T for trust and talking. If you keep talking through minor grievances, it'll prevent molehills becoming mountains. Stay in touch with what each other wants and any updates or changes in direction. You can grow together instead of apart.

> *During sex my wife wants to talk to me.*
> *The other night she called me from a hotel*
> *Rodney Dangerfield*

I is for independence and interests that are separate. Space to still be an individual not just someone's other half.

> *When you are in love with someone, you*
> *want to be near him all the time. Except*
> *when you are out buying things and*
> *charging them to him*
> > *Miss Piggy, as told to Henry Beard in*
> > Miss Piggy's Guide to Life.

O for orgasms. Find out how to have them with each other although these days, it is OK and in fact, only polite for women to occasionally fake them. The lads need some encouragement after the last decade or two. Don't get carried away though, he never fakes his erections.

N is for needs. Make sure you both get a chance to express them and have them acknowledged.

S for surprises. Theatre tickets, a small gift, a weekend away. All the gestures that can make someone feel special, loved and not taken for granted.

H is for his and hers. If you're worried about being taken to the cleaners again make a prenuptial agreement.

> *I believe in marriage but there ain't going*
> *to be no equality. If you want to be equal*
> *with me you can get your own Rolls-*
> *Royce, your own house and your own*
> *million dollars*
> > *Muhammad Ali, 1979*

Well I'm off to the pub dear you coming no okay then see you later don't wait up

I is for important, what is and what isn't. Make your time together a top priority, not shoved to the bottom of the list after work, children, *NYPD Blues*. Well, OK, second on the list after *NYPD Blues*.

P is for partnership and that means some compromise and considering each other's taste in everything from decor to diet. It takes two.

> *When I got married, all the property was put in two names. My wife's. And her mother's*
>
> Rodney Dangerfield

And finally if you do remarry, don't let your past haunt you. Take a tip from Johnny Carson when he said never ask your wife if she stills hears from her old pimp. Let bygones be bygones.

12

ASTROLOGY FOR DIVORCEES

Aries

The randy goat who dives in before thinking about the consequences. No doubt a divorcee because you married too soon or had an affair without thinking.

Our star signs were mis-matched and so were our libidos - I was normal, but she only wanted sex fifteen times a week

Take your time next time and don't leap into the first relationship that comes along.

Taurus

A stubborn old bull. Most likely lost in love because you couldn't step down. Next time agree to disagree sometimes – you're not always right.

Gemini

Schizoid, the sign of the twin and dual personality. Can be two-faced. Most likely you had an affair and got found out.

Next time remember the eleventh commandment. 'Thou shalt not get caught.'

Cancer

A lunatic with a tendency to walk sideways on full moons. A hard shell hides a soft and vulnerable heart that often they are scared to reveal for fear of being hurt.

Live a little, who wants to live with a crabby hard-nut?

Leo

Stop showing off and always wanting to be the centre of attention. Learn to consider and complement new partners or you'll be a lonely old lion.

Virgo

The perfectionist. Your obsessive habits can drive away the most willing of partners. Loosen up a bit, chill out. Learn to leave dinner dishes till the morning and for God's sake stop straightening towels.

Libra

A total ditherer, always weighing up both sides. Make up your mind what you want or you'll be left sitting on the fence forever.

Scorpio

Secretive with a nasty sting stored up to strike. Be nice, smile a little. Nobody likes a bitter old bully.

Sagittarius

Half man, half horse. Try not to let the beast take over all the time or you'll be forever at Alcoholics Anonymous, Narcotics Anonymous or Sex Addicts Anonymous.

Give both parts of you an equal time share.

Capricorn

Capricorn marriages often fail because they are workaholics or working their way up the success ladder and feel they have to trade in old partners for more updated models. Can become a boring old duffer if you don't watch it. Go for Lambada lessons and stop taking it all so seriously.

Aquarius

Sign of the genius. Anyone born under this sign is OK, married, divorced or single. However, many Aquarians are a little absentminded so might not remember *which* they are – married, divorced or single.

Pisces

Idealistic dreamer. Sign of the fish so try not to kiss like a wet one.

They often divorce as partners don't reach their expectations and fall short of their romantic ideals. Get real or it will be a long line of let downs. No one will ever fit the ideal. Go to the movies for that and in your daily life, learn to compromise.

Never play cards with a man called Doc.
Never eat at a place called Mom's. Never
sleep with a woman whose troubles are
worse than yours

Nelson Agren

ANY FINAL TIPS FROM THE PANEL?

Buy Marks and Sparks ready-made dinners, get a cleaner in once a week and masturbate regularly

Stay single

A glass of Bollinger every night with your beloved for surefire marital bliss. But don't let the wife know

Don't go for moody tarts, neurotics, primadonnas, intensely family orientated girls, gold-diggers or whores

Keep trying to find the G spot, it has to be in there somewhere

Always wear a condom

Remember Durex have a sell by date

No one person is ever going to solve your life. You are ultimately here on this planet alone and so never put all your expectations onto someone else. You have to learn to like being alone and happy before you can be with someone else and happy

If at first you don't succeed, try, try, try again

Girl Chasing
How to Improve Your Game

Cathy Hopkins

With cartoons by Gray Jolliffe

For the first time in the history of sex, here is the definitive guide to understanding, charming – and winning – the ladies.

Cathy Hopkins, herself a girl and an expert on the complicated and often puzzling, female psyche, has produced a hilariously entertaining and comprehensive manual for all men who want to play the Girl Chasing Game, with lots of indispensible Game Plan information – how to meet them, flirt with them, interpret their body language, impress them, and even – perish the thought – how to cope with rejection!

ISBN 0 00 637940 0

Man Hunting!

A Girl's Guide to the Game

Cathy Hopkins

With cartoons by Gray Jolliffe

The gentle art of man hunting has been a favourite with females ever since Eve first discovered the power of apples as bait. But never before have the subtleties of the game been so comprehensively chronicled as here. From stalking your prey, to flirting and dating, from keeping him to losing him, this is the most up-to-date guide you'll find to the rules of the game, '90s style, and a lighthearted handbook for the girl who likes to know what she's doing.

ISBN 0 00 638355 6

Henry Beard and Christopher Cerf

Sex and Dating

The Official
Politically Correct Guide

If you thought going on a date was simply a question of spending time with the opposite sex – think again! Dating is a consequence of 'phallocratic social conditioning', and before you indulge in such 'heterocentrism', or even 'consensual love-making', you must learn the language and the rules of the be-sensitive-or-else 1990s.

Only Henry Beard and Christopher Cerf can guide you through the politically correct minefield of sexual etiquette – what to do, where to do it, what to call it, who to do it with, and what they'll do to you if you try. Don't even think about calling your significant other until you've read this informative, hilarious and increasingly topical book.

Romance isn't dead, it's just 'terminally inconvenienced'!

0 00 638377 7

Deborah McKinlay

Love Lies

What Men Don't Know
and Women Won't Admit

A woman has a small part in her brain (about the size of a green pea) which understands that a man who is standing in a room full of business colleagues is NOT likely to say 'I love you too, Bubba, BIG kiss', over the phone.

The rest of her goes into a bit of a huff.

From flowers to foreplay, from going out to staying in, this is the funniest, truest, most hair-raisingly accurate book ever written about relationships since man first looked at woman and said – 'I'll give you a call.' Hysterically funny, toe-curlingly true and altogether indispensable, LOVE LIES is absolutely the last word on love, life and sex in the 1990s.

0 00 638356 4

Please find listed below more humour titles available from HarperCollins:

French For Cats	Henry Beard	0 00 637823 4	£4.99
Advanced French for Exceptional Cats	Henry Beard	0 00 638078 6	£5.99
Official Exceptions to the Rules of Golf	Henry Bead	0 58621843 2	£6.99
The Official Politically Correct Dictionary	Henry Beard	0 586 21726 6	£4.99
Girl Chasing	Cathy Hopkins	0 00 637940 0	£4.50
Keeping It Up	Cathy Hopkins	0 00 637855 2	£4.99
Merde!	Geneviève	0 00 637793 9	£5.99
Merde Encore!	Geneviève	0 00 637785 8	£5.99
Wicked French	Howard Tomb	0 207 16665 X	£2.99
Wicked Italian	Howard Tomb	0 207 16666 8	£2.99
World's Best Business Jokes	Charles Alverson	0 207 16385 5	£2.99
World's Best Drinking Jokes	Ernest Forbes	0 207 16607 2	£3.50
World's Best Marriage Jokes	Ernest Forbes	0 00 637839 0	£3.50
More Golf Jokes	Ernest Forbes	0 00 637934 6	£3.50
World's Best Dirty Limericks	Harold H Hart	0 207 14650 0	£2.99
World's Best Irish Jokes	Des Machale	0 207 14836 8	£2.99
More World's Best Irish Jokes	Des Machale	0 207 15069 9	£2.99
Still More of the World's Best Irish Jokes	Des Machale	0 207 16880 6	£2.99
World's Best Scottish Jokes	Des Machale	0 207 15805 3	£2.99
World's Best Golf Jokes	Robert McCune	0 00 637802 1	£2.99
More of the World's Best Dirty Jokes	Mr J	0 207 14231 9	£2.99
Still More of the World's Best Dirty Jokes	Mr J	0 207 14730 2	£2.99
More World's Best Drinking Jokes	Edward Phillips	0 00 637959 1	£2.99

☐	WORLD'S BEST AFTER-DINNER JOKES Edward Phillips	0-00-637960-5	£2.99
☐	WORLD'S BEST SKIING JOKES Ernest Forbes	0-00-638246-0	£2.99
☐	WORLD'S BEST MOTORING JOKES Edward Phillips	0-00-638265-7	£2.99
☐	WORLD'S BEST BOSS JOKES Edward Phillips	0-00-638241-X	£2.99
☐	WORLD'S BEST DRINKING JOKES Ernest Forbes	0-00-638242-8	£2.99
☐	WORLD'S BEST DIRTY JOKES Mr J	0-00-637784-X	£2.99
☐	WORLD'S BEST FISHING JOKES John Gurney	0-00-637929-X	£2.99
☐	WORLD'S BEST HOLIDAY JOKES Edward Phillips	0-00-637942-7	£2.99
☐	WORLD'S BEST SCOTTISH JOKES Des MacHale	0-00-638264-9	£2.99
☐	WORLD'S BEST LIGHT-BULB JOKES Cathy Hopkins & Edward Phillips	0-00-638461-7	£2.99

All these books are available from your local bookseller or can be ordered direct from the publishers.

To order direct just tick the titles you want and fill in the form below:

Name: _____

Address: _____

_____

Postcode: _____

Send to: HarperCollins Paperbacks Mail Order, Dept 8, HarperCollins *Publishers*, Westerhill Road, Bishopbriggs, Glasgow G64 2QT.

Please enclose a cheque or postal order or your authority to debit your Visa/Access account –

Credit card no: _____

Expiry date: _____

Signature: _____

– to the value of the cover price plus:

UK & BFPO: Add £1.00 for the first and 25p for each additional book ordered.

Overseas orders including Eire, please add £2.95 service charge.

Books will be sent by surface mail but quotes for airmail despatches will be given on request.

24 HOUR TELEPHONE ORDERING SERVICE FOR ACCESS/VISA CARDHOLDERS –

TEL: GLASGOW 0141-772 2281 or LONDON 0181-307 4052